STEVE TERRILL
OREGON
IMAGES OF THE LANDSCAPE

PHOTOGRAPHY BY STEVE TERRILL

WESTCLIFFE PUBLISHERS, INC.   ENGLEWOOD, COLORADO

CONTENTS

International Standard Book Number: ISBN 0-942394-48-8
Library of Congress Catalogue Card Number: 86-051595
Copyright, Photographs and Text: Steve Terrill, 1987
Editor: Scott Lankford
Designer: Gerald M. Simpson/Denver
Typographer: Dianne J. Borneman
Printer: Dai Nippon Printing Company, Ltd.,Tokyo, Japan
Publisher: Westcliffe Publishers, Inc.
2650 South Zuni Street
Englewood, Colorado 80110

Bibliography,   John Muir Quotations

[The source is followed by the page number in this book on which the quotation appears.]

1. "The Forests of Oregon," *Picturesque California* (1888): 16, 22, 32, 86, 138, 150.

2. "Wild Parks and Reservations," *Our National Parks* (1901): 12, 28, 34, 36, 38, 44, 46, 58, 68, 70, 74, 76, 80, 94, 154.

3. *The Mountains of California* (The Century Co., New York, 1894, 1911, 1912):
   "The River Floods": 20, 116.
   "A Near View of the High Sierra": 48, 54, 64, 84, 90, 108, 114, 132, 134.
   "A Wind Storm in the Forest": 96.
   "The Snow": 100, 102, 156.
   "The Glacier Lakes": 106, 128.

4. *Travels in Alaska* (1915): 26, 82, 122, 124, 140, 144, 146.

5. "Twenty Hill Hollow," *Overland Monthly* (April, 1872): 52, 118.

6. "The Alaska Trip," *The Century Magazine* (August, 1897): 60.

7. From *John of the Mountains: The Unpublished Journals of John Muir*, edited by Linnie Marsh Wolfe. Copyright 1938 by Wanda Muir Hanna. Copyright renewed 1966 by John Muir Hanna and Ralph Eugene Wolfe. Reprinted by permission of Houghton Mifflin Company: 148.

First frontispiece: Undulating sands capture shadows and light near Cape Sebastian, southern Oregon coast

Second frontispiece: Mount Jefferson reflects in the pristine waters of Russell Lake, Mount Jefferson Wilderness

Third frontispiece: Autumn leaves ascend stone steps at the foot of Wahkeena Falls, Columbia River Gorge

Title page: Haystack Rock silhouetted in the waning afternoon light, Cannon Beach

Right: Magnolia trunks awash in a sea of fallen petals, Multnomah County

FOREWORD

This book represents the first comprehensive selection ever assembled from John Muir's writings on the state of Oregon and the Northwest. Muir made three journeys to the Pacific Northwest: in 1879 and 1880 while en route to Alaska, and in 1888 while en route to Washington's Mount Rainier. Best known for his writings about the wilderness of California and Alaska, Muir was also deeply influenced by the beauty of Oregon State.

Unlike his famous writings on California and Alaska, Muir's observations about Oregon's wilderness never were published in book form, except as sidetrips in volumes devoted to other locations. By presenting, for the first time in a single volume focused exclusively on Oregon State, a careful selection from his Northwest writings, we hope to help establish John Muir as a foremost—if not the foremost—wilderness poet of the Pacific Northwest.

—Scott Lankford
Program in Modern Thought and Literature
Stanford University

"One day's exposure to mountains is better than cartloads of books. See how willingly nature poses herself upon photographer's plates. No earthly chemicals are so sensitive as those of the human soul."

Thus wrote naturalist John Muir, a man whose personal vision of wilderness imparts to his readers the aesthetic insights of his wide-ranging curiosity. Although Muir was a lover of books who surrounded himself with the writings of poets, philosophers, and naturalists, he knew that only direct contact with nature could nourish the soul. Word-making has its place, but can not make a person feel elemental forces and, in the process, life's deeper meanings.

With a vision similar to Muir's, Steve Terrill has preserved on film these images of Oregon—a distillation of his intimate relationship with the land. Like Muir, he has come to understand nuances of light and form, steeping himself in the mercurial world around him. This is the record of a journey, one guided by an inquiring mind given to looking beyond the obvious with the patience to await the unexpected. It speaks with a poetry both bold and subtle, composed of line, form, color, and light.

Terrill's patient understanding of light is what shapes the cold beauty of his mountain images. It catches the fallen leaves of autumn's restlessness. It delineates woven mosses, shaded branches, and decaying logs. It captures the living tapestry of ivy and fern, luxuriating in the green half-light of Oregon's rain forests. And in the hollows of the forest floor, touched most often by the coolness of shadows, it records the feathery flowers of frost—ephemeral blossoms of the night's chill.

With an attentive eye, Terrill captures Oregon's rapidly changing weather patterns, holding vigil with his camera to catch the sky's ripple of morning fire when altocumulus clouds reflect the sun's hidden light. He focuses his lens on a gathering storm, when an expanding cloud seems to grow as a living thing, feeding on the great currents of the atmosphere until its massive shadow covers the land in a preternatural light. He anticipates the arc of a rainbow, when a retreating wall of rain darkens the distant sky and the rays of a low sun reflect and refract into the familiar bands of colored light.

Always seeking to depict the unusual in the common, Terrill finds beauty in the branching symmetry of a barren oak silhouetted against the coldest sky of winter. In the tangled softness of cottonwood seeds lifted from the mother tree by the breath of spring. In the moth-like fruit of the maple and the winged nutlets of the birch, their airborne clusters a collaboration of tree and wind in a cyclic dance of life. In the scurryings of first snow, when weaving trails of powder flow like ripples in a river's current.

As do Muir's writings, Terrill's photographs record more than the beauty found in nature. They speak of the need to conserve a part of our natural environment—as essential to the soul as water is to the body. "Any fool can destroy trees," Muir once wrote. "They cannot run away; and if they could, they would still be destroyed,—chased and hunted down as long as fun or a dollar could be got out of their bark hides, branching horns, or magnificent bole backbones. Few that fell trees plant them; nor would planting avail much towards getting back anything like the noble primeval forests. . . ."

Were Muir to be transported somehow to present-day Oregon, he would find the land little-changed from when he visited in 1888. Tall stands of Douglas fir and pine still carpet its mountains, lakes and rivers run clear with snow melt, and few humans intrude upon the desert silence where pungent juniper grows.

Oregon has had its share of spokesmen for the preservation of wilderness. Each has added to public awareness of what will be lost—perhaps forever—if the boundaries of the natural world are pushed back much farther. Telling though their words may be, it is the visual experience of what is at stake that strikes the most sensitive chords of our beings. In Terrill's photographs, we see nature in some of her most revealing and beautiful moments.

Accompanying Terrill on a visual journey across the state, we tramp mountain meadows filled with spring's first fertile stirrings. We search summer's woodlands when a thickening canopy of leaves filters the sunlight, imbuing the undergrowth with a lambent richness. We watch fall's gathering of great clouds—fluffy flotillas scudding across the immense dome of sky. We hike the Cascade Range when winter is a cold, white silence across the land.

One of Muir's favorite philosophers, Ralph Waldo Emerson, once wrote, "Such is the constitution of all things, or the plastic power of the human eye, that the primary forms, as the sky, the mountain, the tree, the animal, give us a delight in and for themselves; a pleasure arising from outline, color, motion, and grouping."

In Emerson's day, only the artist with canvas and paints could hope to render some degree of the beauty seen in nature. Today, the camera lens translates the artist's exact vision at the critical instant of revealment. The viewer becomes, in essence, one with the photographer at that moment in time. In this book, there are many such moments, each taking the reader to a time and place of private revelation.

—Brian F. Berger

Eagle Cap's snow-dotted slopes rise above Mirror Lake, Eagle Cap Wilderness

PREFACE

Rocks break loose under my feet and tumble down the steep embankment. What comes to mind is not the danger I'm placing myself in, but the possibility that I may be the first person to have set foot here. An area of near-primeval stillness, broken only by the song of a bird and something rustling in the underbrush. A framework of lush greenery, from which rises the great bulk of Mount Hood.

Such moments of solitude are what have led me to photography in an attempt to capture something of the spiritual essence I feel when submersed in nature. Photographic images preserve that moment when a beam of light parts the clouds, casting an eerie radiance through the forest, emboldening the shadows of towering firs caught in the aura. Or the moment I come upon a meadowland resplendent in wildflowers, their vivid colors drenched by morning dew, a kaleidoscopic oasis amid the variegated woodland greenery. Or when changing light molds and remolds the contours of the mysterious and subtly colored shapes of Oregon's coastal sandstone formations.

In my search of the unrivaled moment, the unique setting, I have explored the nearly 400 miles of Oregon's rugged coastline, where wind-worn cliffs stand like impregnable ramparts against the Pacific's perpetual onslaught. Where inlets and bays shelter intricate tidepools filled with diverse life forms and the ever-present barnacle-encrusted blue mussels. Where sea winds have sculpted a land of sinuous and ephemeral patterns from the undulating sand dunes of the central coast. I have visited the many small towns snugged along this twisting shoreline, each with its own quaint charm and much the same ambiance of a New England village. I have hiked trails that wind through the evergreen forest of the coastal range, searching through a profusion of ferns and mosses to photograph clumps of elusive fungi.

The massive volcanic barrier of the Cascade Range forms a climatic wall between the eastern and western portions of the state. With camera in hand, I have explored its length and breadth. On the west face, rain forest vegetation encloses countless lakes, streams, and waterfalls. An atmosphere of something ancient and undisturbed pervades its deeply shaded forests. Shadows harbor a moisture-laden heaviness, where ferns and lichen flourish and clusters of mushrooms lurk.

Breaching this mountain chain is the great flow of the Columbia River, its waters having formed a gorge of gigantic basaltic cliffs. Looking eastward, the waterway leads to Oregon's drier central and eastern sections. Here is found the drama of the Painted Hills, with their bands of red, gold, green, and black clay. In the dog days of summer, I have watched shifting light on these smooth rolling hills, while nearby cactus bloomed and the pervasive aroma of sagebrush filled the air. I have lingered among the hills while winter dusted their colors with white, resembling some far desert's ancient dunes.

In many ways this is a land of greater contrasts than that found to the west. Here, warm days are followed by cold nights, under skies so intensely black that the Milky Way becomes a visible band of ethereal light. Flatlands give way to lofty buttes and towering cinder cones, and to the sudden intrusion of the Wallowa Mountains of the northeast. Thunderstorms appear and then depart with deceptive quickness. And in the extreme heat of summer and the snows of winter, there is the solitude of vast spaces broken only by a scattering of small towns.

A photographer can anticipate, but can not know. This is what makes photography the adventure it is for me. Each sunrise and sunset holds the unexpected. I have come to know the earth as a canvas, each day painted anew by the

Punch Bowl Falls replenishes Eagle Creek, Columbia River Gorge

subtleties of light that play upon its surface. If I'm lucky, I place my camera in the right spot at the right time to catch the master stroke that completes the picture. If not, I await another day, until the canvas glows with that one masterly image.

Still vividly etched in my memory is one unexpected incident I encountered while collecting images for this book. Accompanied by my son, Steve, and a friend, I was backpacking into the Mount Jefferson Wilderness. We were seeking fields of wildflowers—which I knew to be abundant in the area—hoping to use them as foreground for a photograph of Mount Jefferson.

The hike to Scout Lake had been grueling, as I had overloaded my pack with extra film, food, and clothes in preparation for any eventuality. Ignoring my aches and pains, I took off within minutes of setting up camp to scout the area for wildflowers. The more I searched, the more disappointed I became. I had hoped that the region's many tarns would be sprinkled with a profusion of color, but there were few flowers to be seen. Soon I realized we had arrived two to three weeks early.

The next day I rolled out of bed at 5 a.m., determined to at least photograph a sunrise before packing up and moving on. What greeted me was a landscape devoid of trees; I was immersed in the thickest fog I had ever seen! As I quickly dressed, my mind was working a mile a second, thinking how best to capture the eerie surroundings. Then I remembered some tree-bordered tarns we had passed. If only, I thought, I could photograph Mount Jefferson through the fog from such a setting. Slowly I made my way through the open meadows, fog closing in behind me, shrinking my visible world to a mere 20 feet in all directions. I groped along until I reached a pool about a half-mile from camp.

Quickly I positioned my camera in the direction I knew the mountain to be. The fog was beginning to swirl, giving me faint glimpses of my surroundings, teasing with heightened expectations. But still no mountain, only brief and ghostly outlines of distant trees which held the promise of something greater looming in the background. I had stationed myself on a boulder whose hardness was scarcely felt as I strained to see through the fog. Suddenly, there it was! The outline of the mountain peeking through and above the thinning mist. Before I could take advantage of the brief clearing, in swirled the fog again, thick and opaque as ever. For three more hours the game of hide-and-seek continued. But now I was prepared, and in those fleeting moments when the curtain parted, all thoughts of flowered meadows evaporated. For the mountain's image was mine, moody and magnificent in the luminous light.

This foggy episode is just one of the many climatic dramas I encountered while compiling images for this book. Reflecting back on the endless miles I hiked, winds that nearly blew my camera over, the baking heat of desert country in summer, and hail pelting my face until it ached, I know I would do it all again. For the reward has been a deeper awareness of the natural order of things, and the enjoyment of recording for others these images of the Oregon landscape.

STEVE TERRILL

For my son, Steve, whose encouragement helped transform my dream into reality.

Autumn's chill rimes wild blackberry vines, Multnomah County

COLOR

I look for intense, bold colors that stand out from their surroundings. I also search for subtle shades that blend together yet complement one another. By contrasting at the same time that they conform to their environment, brilliant hues enhance a natural scene. Some landscapes seem almost to jump out at you, appearing for a brief moment to have been painted by an artist, then bringing the realization that nature, indeed, was the creator.

I seek out images with strength and impact, an overpowering feeling that creates a mood and portends seasonal change. A scene resplendent in intense hues of red, yellow, and orange instantly evokes the season of autumn. Shades of white and gray emphasize the harshness of winter, just as a rainbow of color in a field of wildflowers informs the viewer that summer has arrived.

With great anticipation, I point my camera toward sunrises and sunsets, aware that with each passing moment the sky and clouds change rapidly from red to pink, orange, yellow, purple, blue. I am compelled to seek out colors that take authority over a setting. Often I look not only for color in my subject, but for a combination of pattern and color that brings an emotional response from the viewer.

Explosion of fall foliage, Mount Hood National Forest

Flourishing roses encroach upon an abandoned home, Multnomah County

Scarlet cups nestle in a bed of moss and fallen leaves, Columbia River Gorge

"*The countless hosts waving at home beneath their own sky, beside their own noble rivers and mountains, and standing on a flower-enameled carpet of mosses thousands of square miles in extent, attract but little attention.*"

Rhododendron in bloom, Mount Hood National Forest

Oak trees rise above a blanket of flowering balsamroot, Rowena Plateau

"*A*long the lower slopes, especially in Oregon, where the woods are less dense, there are miles of rhododendron, making glorious masses of purple in the spring, while all about the streams and the lakes and the beaver meadows there is a rich tangle of hazel, plum, cherry, crab-apple, cornel, gaultheria, and rubus, with myriads of flowers and abundance of other more delicate bloomers."

Manzanita shrub snakes its way across lichen, Mount Hood

Sodden oak leaves, Multnomah County

"*The rain brought out the colors of the woods with delightful freshness, the rich brown of the bark of the trees and the fallen burs and leaves and dead ferns; the grays of rocks and lichens; the light purple of swelling buds, and the warm yellow greens of the libocedrus and mosses.*"

Autumn's palette streaks across vine maple, Mount Hood National Forest

Indian paintbrush blooms from a rocky outcropping at the foot of Mount Jefferson's northern slope, Mount Jefferson Wilderness

Overleaf: Erosion's artistic creation, Painted Hills, John Day Fossil Beds National Monument

"Surely out of all the abounding forest-wealth of Oregon a few specimens might be spared to the world, not as dead timber, but as living trees. A park of moderate extent might be set apart and protected for public use forever, containing at least a few hundreds of each of these noble pines, spruces, and firs. Happy will be the men who, having the power and the love and benevolent forecast to do this, will do it. They will not be forgotten. The trees and their lovers will sing their praises, and generations yet unborn will rise up and call them blessed."

Phlox wildflowers in passionate bloom, Mount Hood National Forest

Clay rock fragments daubed with pastel hues, Eagle Creek

"*Everybody needs beauty as well as bread, places to play in and pray in where Nature may heal and cheer and give strength to body and soul alike.*"

Duckweed emerges from Timber Lake, Mount Hood National Forest

Grass and duckweed obscure surface of pond, Columbia River Gorge

Overleaf: South Falls arc through the mist, Silver Falls State Park

"*The lower portions of the reserves are solemnly soaked and poulticed in rain and fog during the winter months, and there is a sad dearth of sunshine, but with a little knowledge of woodcraft any one may enjoy an excursion into these woods even in the rainy season. The big, gray days are exhilarating, and the colors of leaf and branch and mossy bole are then at their best. The mighty trees getting their food are seen to be wide-awake, every needle thrilling in the welcome nourishing storms, chanting and bowing low in glorious harmony, while every raindrop and snowflake is seen as a beneficent messenger from the sky.*"

Sun-streaked ripples weave around grasses and rocks in icy tarn,
Mount Jefferson Wilderness

Poppies in riotous bloom, Hood River County

"*Passing from beneath the shadows of the woods where the trees
grow close and high, we step into charming wild gardens full of lilies,
orchids, heathworts, roses, etc., with colors so gay and forming such
sumptuous masses of bloom, they make the gardens of civilization,
however lovingly cared for, seem pathetic and silly.*"

Cobra lily plants curl up from a bog, Lane County, central Oregon coast

Moss finds a home on ponderosa pine trees, Ochoco National Forest

"*These grand reservations should draw thousands of admiring visitors at least in summer, yet they are neglected as if of no account, and spoilers are allowed to ruin them as fast as they like. A few peeled spars cut here were set up in London, Philadelphia, and Chicago, where they excited wondering attention; but the countless hosts of living trees rejoicing at home on the mountains are scarce considered at all.*"

Vine maples revel in autumn's mantle, Willamette National Forest

Rabbitbrush overlooks Cleetwood Cove, Crater Lake National Park

"*The tendency nowadays to wander in wilderness is delightful to see. Thousands of tired, nerve-shaken, over-civilized people are beginning to find out that going home to the mountains is going home; that wildness is a necessity; and that mountain parks and reservations are useful not only as fountains of timber and irrigating rivers, but as fountains of life. Awakening from the stupefying effects of the vice of over-industry and the deadly apathy of luxury, they are trying as best they can to mix and enrich their own little ongoings with those of Nature, and to get rid of rust and disease. . . .*

Weeping willow, Multnomah County

Shadows and light play a duet in the glassy surface of McCord Creek,
Multnomah County

Overleaf: Mount Bachelor's solitary sunrise reflection in Elk Lake,
Deschutes County

"...*Briskly venturing and roaming, some are washing off sins and*
cobweb cares of the devil's spinning in all-day storms on mountains;
sauntering in rosiny pinewoods or in gentian meadows, brushing
through chaparral, bending down and parting sweet, flowery sprays;
tracing rivers to their sources, getting in touch with the nerves of
Mother Earth; jumping from rock to rock, feeling the songs of them,
panting in the whole-souled exercise, and rejoicing in deep,
long-drawn breaths of pure wildness."

FORM

In my eyes, form has a way of bringing a photograph to life, of creating character in a subject. As with many shapes produced by the forces of nature, I accentuate contours and lines with the selective use of light. I search not only for forms that please my eye, but also attempt to capture the illusion of movement in motionless objects.

I attempt to captivate people's minds, then fill them with curiosity as they view forms and contemplate how patterns were created by nature without aid of man. Along the Oregon coast, for instance, I photographed the strangely beautiful sight of smooth, mysteriously shaped sandstone walls embedded with almost-perfectly rounded stones. I also look for patterns within forms that transform a scene into a natural, flowing landscape, such as the shapely, somewhat sensual appearance of sand dunes. Overlaid with ripples created by wind, sand dune designs are accented by the late-evening dance of shadow and light. Certain images can even evoke the sense of touch, so I try to stimulate the senses not only with the beauty of the photograph, but by letting the viewer visually feel the image.

Drawing upon techniques used in black and white photography, I try to capture form without using overpowering colors that might distract the eye. As a result, form, not color, is emphasized. At other times, however, color and form combine for breathtaking images of great impact.

Undulating interplay of sandstone and rocks, Seal Rock Beach

Fog-shrouded alder trees, Columbia River Gorge

Sand scallops await water's return, Sandy River

"*Along the moist, balmy, foggy, west flank of the mountains, facing the sea, the woods reach their highest development, and, excepting the California redwoods, are the heaviest on the continent. They are made up mostly of the Douglas spruce with the giant arbor-vitae, or cedar, and several species of fir and hemlock in varying abundance, forming a forest kingdom unlike any other, in which limb meets limb, touching and overlapping in bright, lively, triumphant exuberance, two hundred and fifty, three hundred, and even four hundred feet above the shady, mossy ground.*"

Bunchberry in bloom atop Bald Mountain, Mount Hood National Forest

Boulder punctuates sandstone design, Shore Acres State Park

"In the autumn berries of every color and flavor abound, enough for birds, bears, and everybody, particularly about the stream-sides and meadows where sunshine reaches the ground: huckle-berries, red, blue, and black, some growing close to the ground, others on bushes ten feet high; gaultheria berries, called 'sal-al' by the Indians; salmon berries, an inch in diameter, growing in dense prickly tangles, the flowers, like wild roses, still more beautiful than the fruit. . ."

Vine maples, Mount Hood National Forest

Icicles pierce a wall of licorice ferns, Columbia River Gorge

Overleaf: Creases of clay and volcanic ash blanketed in snow,
Painted Hills, John Day Fossil Beds National Monument

"*All things were warming and awakening. Frozen rills began to
flow, the marmots came out of their nests in boulder piles and climbed
sunny rocks to bask, and the dun-headed sparrows were flitting about
seeking their breakfasts. The lakes seen from every ridge-top were
brilliantly rippled and spangled, shimmering like the thickets of the
low dwarf pines. The rocks, too, seemed responsive to the vital
heat—rock crystals and snow crystals thrilling alike.*"

Trees and teasels commune in fog, Delta Park, Multnomah County

Still life in drying mud, Multnomah County

" . . .*P*lain, sky, and mountains ray beauty which you feel. You bathe
in these spirit-beams, turning round and round, as if warming at a
camp-fire. Presently you lose consciousness of your own separate
existence: you blend with the landscape, and become part and parcel
of nature."

Log jam of basalt formations, Hood River County

Ramona Falls tumbles to rocks below, Mount Hood Wilderness

Overleaf: Sunset silhouette at Twin Rocks, northern Oregon coast

"*The waterfall sang in chorus, filling the old ice fountain with its solemn roar, and seeming to increase in power as the night advanced—fit voice for such a landscape.*"

Blue shadows in late-evening light, Mount Hood

Yellow bee plants hug valley contours, Painted Hills,
John Day Fossil Beds National Monument

"The icy dome needs none of man's care, but unless the reserve is guarded the flower bloom will soon be killed, and nothing of the forests will be left but black stump monuments."

Sandstone faces survey Shore Acres State Park, Oregon coast

Nature's own popsicles, Horsetail Falls, Columbia River Gorge

Overleaf: Sunset backlights oak trees, Multnomah County

"*Rounded masses of hard, resisting rocks rise everywhere along the shore and in the woods, their scored and polished surfaces still unwasted, telling of a time, so lately gone, when the whole region lay in darkness beneath an all-embracing mantle of ice.*"

Shrouded by clouds, South Sister reflects in Green Lake,
Three Sisters Wilderness

White Mule's Ears in bloom, Big Summit Prairie

"...Going to the mountains is like going home. We always find that
the strangest objects in these fountain wilds are in some degree
familiar, and we look upon them with a vague sense of having seen
them before."

SOFT LIGHT

On an overcast day, clouds act like a huge reflector that casts an even, soft light across the landscape. By subduing the sun's harsh, distracting light, which tends to produce overwhelming shadows, clouds create a uniform light that does not intensify any one object in the photograph. Soft light also tends to bring out the true colors of a subject by eliminating powerful light rays that often intensify an image by exaggerating form and color.

One of the reasons I like photographing in soft light is this tendency for it to capture the true forms, patterns, and colors of nature. I also attempt to bring out the sensitivity of a subject—to create an intimate mood—through the use of soft light. Often I capitalize on the moody, almost romantic, setting that soft light creates. Fog, for instance, can bring peace and harmony to a scene. More often than not, a soft-light image places the viewer at ease. The viewer feels good about the photograph without being overpowered.

Puddle montage of cottonwood, alder, and maple leaves, Hood River County

Paxillus mushrooms emerge from fallen leaves, Columbia River Gorge

Solomon's seal and bleeding heart wildflowers, Clackamas County

"*P*assing beneath the heavy shadows of the woods, almost anywhere
one steps into lovely gardens of lilies, orchids, heathworts, and wild
roses. "

Soft light filters through bigleaf maple trees, Columbia River Gorge

Autumn-tinted vine maple leaves against ferns, Mount Hood

Overleaf: Mist rises from Upper Multnomah Falls, Columbia River Gorge

"In a few favored spots the broad-leafed maple grows to a height of a
hundred feet in forests by itself, sending out large limbs in magnificent
interlacing arches covered with mosses and ferns, thus forming lofty
sky-gardens, and rendering the underwoods delightfully cool. No finer
forest ceiling is to be found than these maple arches, while the floor,
ornamented with fall ferns and rubus vines, and cast into hillocks by
the bulging, moss-covered roots of the trees, matches it well."

Warm Springs River on a cold day, Warm Springs Indian Reservation

Fluid movement along Camp Creek, Mount Hood National Forest

"*Beside all these bloomers there are wonderful ferneries about the many misty waterfalls, some of the fronds ten feet high, others the most delicate of their tribe, the maidenhair fringing the rocks within reach of the lightest dust of the spray, while the shading trees on the cliffs above them, leaning over, look like eager listeners anxious to catch every tone of the restless waters.*"

Dead manzanita shrub returns to the earth, Mount Hood Wilderness

Rock and sand design near Cape Sebastian, Curry County

Overleaf: Aspen grove, Hood River County

"None of Nature's landscapes are ugly so long as they are wild; and much, we can say comfortingly, must always be in great part wild, particularly the sea and the sky, the floods of light from the stars, and the warm, unspoilable heart of the earth, infinitely beautiful, though only dimly visible to the eye of imagination."

Covered bridge dwarfed by advancing trees,
North Fork of the Yachats River, Lincoln County

Lupine, Indian paintbrush, and butterweed weave a wildflower
tapestry across Summit Meadow, Mount Hood

"*B*ack in the untrodden wilderness a deep furred carpet of brown
and yellow mosses covers the ground like a garment, pressing about
the feet of the trees, and rising in rich bosses softly and kindly over
every rock and mouldering trunk, leaving no spot uncared for."

*Early-morning fog embraces Samuel H. Boardman State Park,
southern Oregon coast*

Roaring River, Willamette National Forest

"*The scenery of the ocean, however sublime in vast expanse, seems
far less beautiful to us dry-shod animals than that of the land seen
only in comparatively small patches; but when we contemplate the
whole globe as one great dewdrop, striped and dotted with continents
and islands, flying through space with other stars all singing and
shining together as one, the whole universe appears as an infinite
storm of beauty.*"

Winter blankets Smith Rock State Park, Deschutes County

Death finds beauty in branches of Douglas fir, Mount Hood National Forest

"*Somber peaks, hacked and shattered, circled halfway around the horizon, wearing a savage aspect in the gloaming, and a waterfall chanted solemnly across the lake on its way down from the foot of a glacier. The fall and the lake and the glacier were almost equally bare; while the scraggy pines anchored in the rock-fissures were so dwarfed and shorn by storm-winds that you might walk over their tops. In tone and aspect the scene was one of the most desolate I ever beheld. But the darkest scriptures of the mountains are illumined with bright passages of love that never fail to make themselves felt when one is alone.*"

Fog-filtered bear grass, Larch Mountain

Wildflower tableau of penstemon and Indian paintbrush,
Mount Hood National Forest

Overleaf: Succor Creek weaves through rock formations, Malheur County

"*Around the great, fire-mountains, above the forests and beneath
the snow, there is flowery zone of marvelous beauty planted with
anemones, erythroniums, daisies, bryanthus, kalmia, vaccinium,
cassiope, saxifrages, etc., forming one continuous garden fifty or sixty
miles in circumference, and so deep and luxuriant and closely woven
it seems as if Nature, glad to find an opening, were economizing space
and trying to see how many of her bright-eyed darlings she can get
together in one mountain wreath.*"

Fog descends on Douglas fir, Mount Hood National Forest

Bracken ferns border Still Creek, Mount Hood National Forest

"*The peaks marshaled along the summit were in shadow, but through every notch and pass streamed vivid sunfire, soothing and irradiating their rough, black angles, while companies of small, luminous clouds hovered above them like very angels of light.*"

PLACE

To perceive place is to capture and express the mood or atmosphere of a particular location. A sense of place sends forth a feeling that lets viewers become a part of the scene by drawing them into the photograph or by inspiring them to want to journey there. By conveying an impression of actually being there, by creating an emotional response to the area, a photograph almost allows viewers to smell the wildflowers or feel the damp sweep of fog wet their faces.

Photographing a relatively minute section of a landscape—such as a wildflower-lined stream—can convey a sense of the surrounding terrain. Occasionally I search for a focal point of interest that captures the imagination without making the eye want to wander. By eliminating distraction or confusion, the photograph evokes a feeling of wonderment or mystery.

I find it challenging to aim my camera at popular, highly photographed areas, to capture a scene or a mood with fresh eyes. Success comes when people viewing the photograph say they recognize the scene but have never seen it in quite the same way. As a photographer, my goal is to enlighten viewers with the hope of opening up their minds and eyes so they can discover more diverse ways to look upon a scene.

Seaweed and sandstone labyrinth, Seal Rock

Fog- and fern-drenched forest, Larch Mountain

Slanting light illuminates rabbitbrush and snow-capped Mount Jefferson

"*The snow that falls on the lower woods is mostly soft, coming through the trees in downy tufts, loading their branches, and bending them down against the trunks until they look like arrows, while a strange muffled silence prevails, making everything impressively solemn. But these lowland snowstorms and their effects quickly vanish. The snow melts in a day or two, sometimes in a few hours; the bent branches spring up again, and all the forest work is left to the fog and the rain.*"

Strawberry Mountains reign over Logan Valley, Grant County

Crumbling granite along shore of Douglas Lake, Eagle Cap Wilderness

Overleaf: Morning light on Mount Jefferson, Mount Jefferson Wilderness

"We hear much nowadays concerning the universal struggle for existence, but no struggle in the common meaning of the word was manifest here; no recognition of danger by any tree; no deprecation; but rather an invincible gladness as remote from exultation as from fear."

*North Sister and Middle Sister from behind a manzanita shrub,
Three Sisters Wilderness*

Elowah Falls, Columbia River Gorge

"*Detached torrents and avalanches from the main wind flood
overhead were rushing wildly down the narrow side cañons, and over
the precipitous walls, with loud resounding roar, rousing the pines to
enthusiastic action, and making the whole valley vibrate as though it
were an instrument being played.*"

Early-morning light hits the southern rim of Crater Lake,
Crater Lake National Park

Frozen cattail creates pond pattern, Mount Jefferson Wilderness

Overleaf: Fog-drenched bear grass and rhododendron,
Mount Hood National Forest

"*Some of these unfortunate lakelets are not clear of ice and snow
until near the end of summer. . . . The frontal cliffs are in some
instances quite picturesque, and with the berg-dotted waters in front of
them lighted with sunshine are exceedingly beautiful. It often happens
that while one side of a lake basin is hopelessly snow-buried and
frozen, the other, enjoying sunshine, is adorned with beautiful flowers.*"

Aspen rise from a blanket of flowering fireweed, Steens Mountain

Mount Hood reflects amid lilies in Multorpor Fen

"Their waters are keen ultramarine blue in the deepest parts, lively grass-green toward the shore shallows and around the edges of the small bergs usually floating about them. A few hardy sedges, frost-pinched every night are occasionally found making soft sods along the sun-touched portions of their shores, and when their northern banks slope openly to the south, and are soil-covered, no matter how coarsely, they are sure to be brightened with flowers."

Celestial spray from Upper Horsetail Falls, Columbia River Gorge

*Resplendent portents of winter at the base of Mount Jefferson,
Mount Jefferson Wilderness*

Overleaf: Rocky remnants of man, Malheur County

"*How truly glorious the landscape circled around this noble
summit!—giant mountains, valleys innumerable, glaciers and
meadows, rivers and lakes, with the wide blue sky bent tenderly over
them all. But in my first hour of freedom from that terrible shadow,
the sunlight in which I was lying seemed all in all.*"

MOMENT

Moments have a way of bringing out the most powerful emotions within me. They thrust deep into my soul to bring out the driving force of determination to combat the elements of nature that I encounter on my photographic excursions. I will endure mile upon mile of hiking trail in the hope of capturing that one precise yet elusive moment in time. A chill of excitement travels the length of my body as I speculate that I may very well be the only person on earth to view this magnificent scene, knowing that this moment will never repeat itself in the same way I have just viewed it.

What fascinates me and what I look for in those special moments of time are the unique blendings of nature's energies that transform an ordinary scene into a personality unmatched anywhere else in the world. On nature's stage, scenes have the ability to change suddenly and, more often than not, with great impact. Rains cut loose from swollen overhead clouds, the sun breaks through a rent in the heavens, and, for one brief moment, sun combined with rain casts a brilliant rainbow that contrasts against an ominous sky. A downpour creates a flash flood, which transforms a once-dry creekbed into a rushing torrent colored by the rich hues of the surrounding soil. In the sky, ever-changing cloud patterns combine with the sunset's hues to create exceptional forms and colors that will never be duplicated.

Frequently I feel like a hunter in search of his prey, stalking and waiting for the perfect shot. For hours at a time, I will sit rooted in the same spot, my camera poised. Relying on intuition and past experience, I wait, knowing full well that my patience will be rewarded with a sudden transformation, the fleeting appearance of that special moment.

Confluence of muddy creeks at Painted Hills,
John Day Fossil Beds National Monument

Mount Hood greets dawn from Blue Lake Park, Multnomah County

Fog drifts toward blooming penstemon and paintbrush,
Mount Hood National Forest

"How glorious a greeting the sun gives the mountains! To behold
this alone is worth the pains of any excursion a thousand times over.
The highest peaks burned like islands in a sea of liquid shade. Then the
lower peaks and spires caught the glow, and long lances of light,
streaming through many a notch and pass, fell thick on the frozen
meadows."

Alder tree reflects through fog, Washington County

Wintry surf near Cape Meares, northern Oregon coast

"*Storms are fine speakers, and tell all they know, but their voices of lightning, torrent, and rushing wind are much less numerous than the nameless still, small voices too low for human ears; and because we are poor listeners we fail to catch much that is fairly within reach. . . . Yet we may draw enjoyment from storm sounds that are beyond hearing, and storm movements we cannot see. The sublime whirl of planets around their suns is as silent as raindrops oozing in the dark among the roots of plants.*"

Foggy reflections in tarn, Mount Hood National Forest

Cloud banks forming above the Walls of Rome, Malheur County

Overleaf: Wintry sunburst over Still Creek, Mount Hood National Forest

"The ordinary rainstorm of this region has little of that outward pomp and sublimity of structure so characteristic of the storms of the Mississippi Valley. Nevertheless, we have experienced rainstorms out on these treeless plains, in nights of solid darkness, as impressively sublime as the noblest storms of the mountains."

Surf pounds Shore Acres State Park, Oregon coast

Alpine tarn in fog, Mount Jefferson Wilderness

"*The waves from the deep Pacific, driven by the gale, broke in a grand display of foam on these bald, hardy islets, leaping over them, at a height of a hundred feet perhaps, in magnificent curving sheets, jagged-edged and flame-shaped, draping the rocks with graceful folds of foam-lace from top to bottom, through the meshes of which the black rock showed in striding contrast, and brought the white lacework ever wasting, ever renewed, into relief. . . .*"

Explosion of water draws scant attention from gulls, Lincoln County

Moonrise over abandoned homestead, Wasco County

Overleaf: Eagle Cap's pristine reflection in Sunshine Lake,
Eagle Cap Wilderness

"*. . .I gazed enchanted as long as they were in sight, watching the exultant, triumphant gestures of the tireless breaking waves, and the explosive upspringing and gentle overarching of the white, purple-tinged foam and spray, sifted with sunshine and fashioned by the wind. How calm and peaceful and graceful they were, combined with tremendous displays of power!—a truly glorious show, however common, and a glorious song.*"

Mount Jefferson and alpine tarn in fog, Mount Jefferson Wilderness

Clouds paint the sky above Mitchell Point, Columbia River Gorge

"*The landscape, cold and bare, is reflected in [a mountain lake's] pure depths; the winds ruffle its glassy surface, and the sun fills it with throbbing spangles, while its waves begin to lap and murmur around its leafless shores,—sun-spangles during the day and reflected stars at night its only flowers, the winds and the snow its only visitors.*"

MICROCOSM AND INFINITY

Many of us tend to ignore the minute world of microcosms as we observe earth's panoramic landscapes. This often-overlooked world-within-a-world is probably my favorite domain of nature photography. I quest for the unique character of the lines, forms, textures, designs, and colors of these miniature landscapes. My camera beholds the delicate products of nature's workmanship alongside the sometimes-chaotic patterns and forms produced by the forces of nature.

Achieving the right mood and feeling often requires a second trip to capture the interplay of seasonal or atmospheric conditions that transforms the image into a work of art. Droplets of rain engulfing a stand of mushrooms, a thin covering of frost lining autumn-tinged leaves, early spring growth emerging through the decaying cover of the forest floor. To emphasize the details of this most intricate realm of nature, I utilize early-morning and late-evening light, and the even lighting of overcast days.

Man finds it difficult to conceive of the far outreaches of infinity as he gazes toward the stars, for man has not yet learned where the universe begins or ends. In much the same way, man's curiosity is stirred when looking down from a mountain to a stand of evergreens woven into a carpet of greenery that extends to distant hills on the horizon. Man realizes that these hills and forests will end somewhere beyond the horizon, but where? To further stimulate man's mind into perceiving infinity, the photographer shifts the camera to include an uninterrupted sky of cottony white clouds in this seemingly endless landscape.

To achieve this sense of infinite regions, I often open photographs with a strong foreground, then lead viewers into the image, drawing their imaginations to distant subjects at horizon's edge. My aim is to engage emotions, to touch inner consciousness, to give birth to an awareness that we are but small life forms amid the vast open realm of nature.

Rainbow's end at Big Indian Creek Gorge, Steens Mountain

Indian paintbrush, Mount Hood National Forest

Wizard Island at sunrise, Crater Lake National Park

"No evangel among all the mountain plants speaks Nature's love more plainly than cassiope. Where she dwells, the redemption of the coldest solitude is complete. The very rocks and glaciers seem to feel her presence, and become imbued with her own fountain sweetness."

Eagle Cap from remote viewpoint, Eagle Cap Wilderness

Horsetail ferns radiate miniature galaxies, Columbia Gorge

Overleaf: The day's waning light sets a sea stack on fire at Cannon Beach,
Oregon coast

"*But, generally, when looking for the first time from an
all-embracing standpoint like this, the inexperienced observer is
oppressed by the incomprehensible grandeur, variety, and abundance
of the mountains rising shoulder to shoulder beyond the reach of
vision; and it is only after they have been studied one by one, long and
lovingly, that their far-reaching harmonies become manifest. . . .
Nature's poems carved out on table of stone—simplest and most
emphatic of her glacial compositions.*"

Dead moths litter pond, Mount Jefferson Wilderness

*Iris blooms against a backdrop of northern inside-out flowers,
Clackamas County*

"... When an excursion into the woods is proposed, all sorts of
exaggerated or imaginary dangers are conjured up, filling the kindly,
soothing wilderness with colds, fevers, Indians, bears, snakes, bugs,
impassable rivers, and jungles of brush, to which is always added
quick and sure starvation."

Sword fern and lichen assault basalt cliff, Columbia River Gorge

Mount Washington dips its reflection in Big Lake, Willamette National Forest

Overleaf: Winter-frosted rock cotoneaster, Multnomah County

"Never before this had I been embosomed in scenery so hopelessly beyond description. To sketch picturesque bits, definitely bounded, is comparatively easy—a lake in the woods, a glacier meadow, or a cascade in its dell. . .

Crooked River winds through Smith Rock State Park, Deschutes County

Western ragweed consumes field, Multnomah County

"...Or even a grand master view of mountains beheld from some commanding outlook after climbing from height to height above the forests. These may be attempted, and more or less telling pictures made of them ...

Starfish convene in tidepools flanked by mussels and barnacles, Depoe Bay

Wave patterns and coastal fog, southern Oregon coast

"*...But in these coast landscapes there is such indefinite, on-leading expansiveness, such a multitude of features without apparent redundance, their lines graduating delicately into one another in endless succession, while the whole is so fine, so tender, so ethereal, that all penwork seems hopelessly unavailing.*"

Mosaic of phlox, Washington County

The Pinnacles standing guard, Crater Lake National Park

" ... *The crest of the Cascades with its grand beacon lights of volcanic cones, now cool in ice and snow eternal.*"

Forest landscape littered with Douglas fir cones, Mount Hood

Lomatium in bloom, Hood River County

Overleaf: Waterlilies in Woahink Lake,
Oregon Dunes National Recreation Area

" *...It was in the Umpqua Hills that this noble tree was first
discovered by the enthusiastic botanical explorer David Douglas, in
the year 1826. This is the Douglas for whom the noble Douglas spruce
is named, and many a fair blooming plant also, which will serve to
keep his memory fresh and sweet as long as beautiful trees and flowers
are loved.* "

Fall flood of vine maples, Mount Hood National Forest

Lady ferns confer with red elderberry, Larch Mountain

"*Picturesque detached groups of the spiry* Abies lasiocarpa *stand like islands along the lower margin of the garden zone, while on the upper margin there are extensive beds of bryanthus, cassiope, kalmia, and other heathworts, and higher still saxifrages and drabas, more and more lowly, reach up to the edge of the ice. Altogether this is the richest subalpine garden I ever found, a perfect floral elysium.*"

South Sister reflects her face in Sparks Lake, Deschutes County

*Cottonwood tree seeds weave a filmy veil around redstem storksbill
wildflowers, Columbia River Gorge*

*Overleaf: Receding waters leave their imprint near Cape Sebastian,
southern Oregon coast*

"*In bold relief, like a clear painting, appeared a most imposing
scene. Innumerable peaks, black and sharp, rose grandly into the dark
blue sky, their bases set in solid white, their sides streaked and
splashed with snow, like ocean rocks with foam; and from every
summit, all free and unconfused, was streaming a beautiful silky
silvery banner, from half a mile to a mile in length, slender at the point
of attachment, then widening gradually as it extended from the peak . . .
there was not a single cloud in the sky to mar their simple grandeur.*"

TECHNICAL
INFORMATION

The images within this book were made with a Linhof Technika 4x5 field view camera, using lenses of 75mm, 90mm, 135mm, 150mm, 270mm, and 360mm focal lengths.

Ektachrome 64 transparency film was used exclusively. An 81B filter was used in cloudy and shaded conditions to correct for an imbalance related to the blue dyes in the film. At times a polarizing filter was used to reduce or eliminate glare.

Exposures were calculated with a Gossen Luna-Pro at 15 and 7.5 degrees. Apertures varied from f5.6 to f64. Exposures varied from 1/100 second to about 90 seconds.

The transparencies were separated on state-of-the-art laser scanning equipment. Color reproduction was achieved with the goal of faithfully duplicating the image on film and accurately capturing the moment as it existed in time.

Owyhee River, Malheur County